MAD BOB REPUBLIC:

Bloodlines, Bile and a Crying Child

struggle poems

Tendai Rinos Mwanaka

Mwanaka Media and Publishing Pvt Ltd,
Chitungwiza Zimbabwe

Creativity, Wisdom and Beauty

Publisher:

Mmap

Mwanaka Media and Publishing Pvt Ltd

24 Svosve Road, Zengeza 1

Chitungwiza Zimbabwe

mwanaka@yahoo.com

https//mwanakamediaandpublishing.weebly.com

Distributed in and outside N. America by African Books Collective

orders@africanbookscollective.com

www.africanbookscollective.com

ISBN: 978-0-7974-9552-4

EAN: 9780797495524

© Tendai Rinos Mwanaka 2018

DISCLAIMER

All views expressed in this publication are those of the author and do not necessarily reflect the views of *Mmap*.

Table of Contents

Introduction

I wrote the poems in this collection in 2008 at the height of Zimbabwe's political problems and they were published in my maiden book, *Voices From Exile*, in 2010, by *Lapwing Poetry, Ireland*. 10 years later we are Full Square to One; we are back in Zimbabwe's endless political problems, as we head towards another election.

A lot has gone down in the last 10 years. The players have changed, but the game seems to be the same, so these poems being republished in their original title I had written them under, *Mad Bob Republic*, highlights the same problems that still bedevil this beautiful country that lies between two great Southern rivers, Limpopo and Zambezi.

Vote rigging, voter apathy, intimidations, biased reporting, hubristic political leaders, political gerrymandering, confused world, tired and timid electorate, and add to this the decay or death of every governance system or structure in Zimbabwe, top this with an economy that is all but dead; These are issues the poems in this collection still address. Is there an end to Zimbabwe's problems? There is no conclusive solution on the horizon now, other than keeping trying and fighting on. This is an addition to the discourses ongoing about the country; this is how I fight as a writer and poet.

Mad Bob Republic is a trimmed offering than *Voices From Exile*; it has 48 poems written in the sudden, unflinching, brutal way- it hammer hits from the first poem to the last one. The focus is on Zimbabwe, which I call *Mad Bob Republic*, the mad Bob is no other than Robert Mugabe, who had taken the country to ransom, making us his private garden he can do whatever the hell he wants with it.

He is gone; he left our political landscape in a soft coup last year. Maybe someday I will bring myself to address the coup in a writing, in relation to post-2018 election dispensation, this book's focus is to use the past to shine a light to our present. The future will come and we will address it accordingly. And as I noted in an essay, *The Portrait Of* in *Zimbabwe: The Blame* it will take a long time to really weed him out of our psyche. Did he really leave, the poem *Did You Say Goodbye To Us*, still asks the same question. Is *Mugabeism* gone? The poems highlights the *Mugabeisms* to answer the questions we might want to ask, the answers are in the interpretations to the poems, the answers lies in Zimbabwe's ability to move forward after this election and heal and become successful again

Poems

BRUTAL TIMES

The arrest and slammed doors
In a cell, in Harare
The beatings, gorging, chopping
In the throes of a shape-shift-
The walls of my cell, in Chikurubi
Maximum prison.
Slanting backwards with weights-
Of a cracked head, gorged flesh and chopped-
Limbs of my own body.
And my steady howling and gnashing cries.

The C.I.O's beatings, questions,
Sexual and psychological abuse
Trying to bleed answers from me.
Also from my next cell's occupant.
Talk, talk, talk, the insistent hammer
Of those words repeated again and again.
Where are your handlers? Where are the weapons?
What was the plan… that I never had?
That I never knew of, and in the next cell-
The green bombers rage at the cell's occupant.

My lawyer asked for bail and for
A doctor to look at my wounds.
Which I was granted by the court, but which
The police defied the court over
And re-locked me back in my cell as

They appeal, re-appeal, and re-appeal the appealed
Judgments, whilst
The beatings continue.
Now timed like eating times, three times
A day like breakfast, lunch and supper.

I didn't have anything more to say
I didn't even have the power to say anything
To admit to the wrongs I knew I hadn't done.
But by the time I had decided to lie
And admit to shelter myself from the beatings
They were now tired of bleeding me out.
So they brought me before the Judge
And I knew that I was a free-man
That Judge Makarau will not find fault
Save for my rotting chopped hands.

They charged me falsely with
Banditry, terrorism, and insurgency
And I was facing a death sentence.
But my lawyer agued long and reasoned
And the judge saw through their schemes
Games and brutalities and-
She released me scotch-free but with-
A brutalized heart, brutalized flesh.
Brutalized soul, brutalized dreams
And brutalized prayers.

But I only felt sorry for-

My next cell's occupant.
Who still had to face more beatings and
Cut limbs before the judge releases him.
Before the CIO tell the police not to-
Appeal, re-appeal---, the judge's decisions.
Before the CIO break his spirit.
Never again to write and say-
Anything against this brutal regime.
Or about its brutalities.

AND THEN

The year I saw her in the distances
  She gave me a long stare.
   That day she blamed me-
    For running out of the country.
     Away from her-
      Down Masvingo road like an insult.

That she found the road curving,
  Into her heart with a condoning-
   Memory-shaft.
    Sorrows opening her eyes to,
     Pain and hurt's mixed bag.

And I knew then that my debt-
  Was impossible to fulfil.
   For the life she had given me, the wounds-
    she bandaged, the medicine, the meals,
     Clothing and a home.
      The sun-rich room of melting smells-
       Heaven-scents of an escaping stream.

But now I can be able to tell her-
  The stories of Chikurubi maximum,
   Prison's combat wars.
    From the days of a brutalized life.

PARAMETERS OF MUGABE'S MIND

My people laugh at me
just to taunt me!
Obama looks at me through
Bush's warmongering eyes
More taunting!

I clip one person
and those western bigots curses me
and we grind across disagreements
but I am not moved by their angers.

We have been at it
for over three decades.
But once again
I must postpone victory
in the face of this onslaught.

I clip another person
no guilty attached, really!
It's a price a country pays
for flaunting its displeasures
against its leader!

Because these people
are possessed of a higher threshold
of tenacity, and dislikes me so much.
Always going against my wishes!

Cursing, cringing, sighing
Fighting and crying-
and digging-in deeper.
Fighting their own leader!

But I can always fall back
into making martyrs again.
knee-deep drifting into
Chinese multiplying tortures.

And I shall kill that toad
who tried to sell my country
to his western friends.
By giving it back to those
bloody homo-rhodesiansies
in Brisbane, London and Joburg.

WRONG TURN

Going the wrong way
never thinking of backing out. His wife comes to him
with a frying pan.

And it never crosses her mind
that she could back out. Light creeps in on her
wherever she wasn't.

A JOURNEY TO NYADZONYA

Did I say goodbye as I left for
Nyadzonya camp?

But now I am scanning the land
and I am on top of the mountain-of-gold-
weeping-tears-and-an-old-man's-beards.

To my left are clusters of a farm
and the land is with bare bushes.

Ahead are a couple of thatched huts
and mango trees are heavy with fruits.

And a little further is Nyadzonya camp-
two storey tall, white-some buildings.

I wonder what your white-some mother was
thinking of as he bombed the place into rubble

and that day, you were a colour red
Nyadzonya River,
now you are green sewerage.

Across are a couple of shacks, for-
shops, and further, more thatched-
huts, and then I see it.

9

Red, black, green, white, yellow
and a star, one star on a Zimbabwean bird.

Flying in the sun, unconcerned
of its own foreignness in this land.

It is a herald to a place
where so many thoughts, so many bones
so much blood and flesh
was made to end in one mass grave.

When I arrive at this place
I look around for my brother
who was to meet me here.

among those thousands, unaccounted-
of my countrymen.

DID YOU SAY GOODBYE TO US?

One of your friends, Pohamba
touches your olding skin.
Your skin with its beautiful scars-
scars of all those Mozambique years.
Nyadzonya, Chimoi, Tembwe, are
wounds on your beautiful old skin.
Maybe your skin reminds you of
those years and how good you felt.

Walking the bloody-fields of Nyadzonya
calling on your donkey or it
might have helped you to think
so clearly as you did.
Did you think, once, then
of the vast collective concerns
of your follower's time?

Though it's your final days.
We laugh but it must feel to you
like the war is still going-on.
As you absorb your last
empty ten decades and fold inside.
Did you say goodbye to us?

MY ENEMIES

My enemies surround me
country by country filled
by Chematama's sympathisers.

They invade my tiny world and
like Europe's maggots bacteria
they reproduce, even when I am asleep
and I wake up to more and more
than from the night before.

And they remind me
that I need to open up
and furnish them with my thinking
paste my feelings into their hearts.
But emotions are always a problem!

Because they protest and shout at me.
That they can only be supplanted on my enemies
through the process
of my own fateful destruction.
But I do not want to die yet,
but to swim in poems and poems
and I am beginning to hate poems.

THAT CHILD

That child still puts on a happy face.
But I like the one she had a decade ago-
For a decade-old smile,
Looks a lot better-
Than this up-to-date happy face.

And I fell in love with that child,
When she showed me the scars-
On her back from beatings,
She received for carrying a flier,
In a comatose nation.
Down through Julius Nyerere way-
On her protests to Monomutapa hotel.

Where are they now, wasting days?
And nights lying to each other,
And to the feared British and Americans
Of a deal. A GNU deal, to deal with-
The things she was protesting against.

And all that I could tell her then was:
A flier is a measure of "acts of terrorism",
If you live in an autocrat's den.
And that if you toss an open palm into midair-
Don't take time to count the stars in the sky,
But follow small ways leading out.

And I couldn't look directly into her heart,
To see the things they had done to her.

HIS PLEASURE

He doesn't-
care. It's not his-
problems, his pleasure!
That late afternoon as-
they scatter out,
and left for-

Wherever they could go.

COMICAL MUSIC

Questions edging conversations
conversations swallowed by
the whispers.

of the earth's murmurings
in comical music.

"He is a modern-day Hitler."
"Bakassa, Mobuto, Idi combined."
"He is mad, Mad Bob is mad."
"He has killed thousands."
"Millions are in dire danger and hunger."
"And millions have left their country."

MY BRIEF STINT AS A TERRORIST

A mindless rage has consumed me
  No, no, no!
I have had enough of this-
  MUGABE, MUGABE, MUGABE,
This and Mugabe that.
  I am tired of hearing the same story-
The same old story.
  And suddenly killing seems a small irrelevancy,
To the interior happenings-
  Inside the country of my brains.

I had been planning for this,
  In my thoughts, a couple of-
Weeks back.
  So there is this friend of mine who stays-
In Soweto, in Kliptown.
  I had gone there to see him, and
I returned back with a
  .38 service revolver and
A couple rounds of bullets.

Then I pack a couple of clean
  Shirts and pants.
The revolver and the bullets
  And leave for Zimbabwe.
And a couple of days later here I am
  Outside Harare, only that

I have never left my room
  In an East Rand ghetto suburb.

It's only my thoughts that are
  In this favrashi of existence.
Did I think, for a moment that
  I could kill Mugabe. Yes!
I will wait for him, across,
  Norton road, lying on my stomach.
I know that he is spending most of-
  His time in Kutama nowadays.
And that he would pass through
  On his way to Harare from Kutama.

I also know the car to shoot today.
  And it would be that-
Second black Mercedes Benz car, and
  I see the motorcade coming through
Into my foci, and I raise
  That wobbly shot-gun.
Eager for my first big;
  Terrorist bang!

'SHOOT THAT CAR!' my thoughts points
  and I sight down the barrel and
I am no longer thinking.
  But I am seeing my target moving before me
And I close one eye and
  I pull the trigger.

And I hear a deafening report.
  Like an old drum being beaten.

The burning barrel ahead of me
  Right at the tyres, dead centre, and
The rising, lifting, car into the air-
  Fire, ash, dust and smoke.
And when I question my thoughts,
  Whether I thought I could do it?
They thought I couldn't have done it.

MILK WITH MARVIN, MY CAT

I gave Marvin some milk to drink
But she just smelled it
And refused to drink it.

I spoke of the D.R.C
But she just stared at me.
I spoke of the elections in Nigeria and Kenya
She started jumping up and down the table.

I spoke of Zimbabwe's problems
She stopped, and stared at me again.
I said it is all because of Mugabe
She just smiled at me like some elfin child.

I spoke of South Africa
And of how Jacob Zuma is good for this country.
She started mewing and growling
And moved out of the room.

And I thought it must have been-
The smell of the milk.

Or Marvin had turned into an Afro-sceptic?

UNITY GOVERNMENT

Unity government is a watercolour government
It is a government that's home to
Ministers and ministries without power
Like coded storylines of untested identity
Within the within is the same, only smaller here
It is its absolute refusal to doubt itself
That hustles us along to our hazardous fringes
Little by little, the big black lies
Strangling the music of our hopes

It is the oppressor's music ruminating in
The vestiges of our now clogged minds
Stories of false hope bound together
In stoic controversies and contradictions
By two actors seeking out unearned recognition
Leading us astray is this liberal hypocrisy
Just a dialectical change

Hope in Zimbabwe is knit with lives lost
And plaited into a pattern of suffering
Hope afraid of unbraiding the past
Waits for others to undo the knots
The unmaking of our old pains
Whose intricate designs and clever joints
We have mistakenly re-knotted again
Hope acts the fool here, don't see
Or we don't want to believe what we are seeing

In Harare north, they still swim in harmless pools
Designing for our dreams
We swim in hunger drenched streets of Chitungwiza
Here they only listen for our voices of dissent
For if they hear us they would kill us with their guns
So we now talk silently like the empty skies
Our very bones hears the sounds of our silent weeping

Each night the empty plates from which we eat
Will be the fields from which you will harvest
New harvests without the words "silent diplomacy."
And at night we crash into nightmares, thinking
That this deck of misfortune that we have re-created
Would keep shoving us to keep fighting
For the horizons are still ours
But we wish the sun would soften a thousand times over

Unity government is just what it is
Or pieces of what it should be
It is the way you live within it
That makes it unworkable for you
As if it's a map you can read only once
But feel like you have read it many times
Because you cannot forget it
Whether you want to, or not

It is stinking masks of skeletons full of odour
It is a street-named "government of national unity."

On a broken down stage called "Zimbabwe."
It is like bits of old jokes without the laughter
But snarls like jumbled half-bars of remembered music

It is just an illusion, a dilution process
So let's not shift our minds in reverse
Let's not fall prey to this new resurrection
A master's rendition, a repetition of 1987
Just another history waiting to be re-written
Through another trough of empty spaces of time.

JOURNEY TO SOUTH AFRICA

We have become raven's baggage
So we call out like a raven
In raven's two voices
Fevered breath or our own wounded feeling

Our nightmares starts
Out of "there is no cholera in Zimbabwe"
Out of the dead men from cholera
Out of the dead women from HIV Aids
Out of the dead children from hunger
Out of the dead young adults from political killings
Out of little children become war soldiers
Out of the vengeance of Mugabe's CIO
Out of the beast ZANU-PF, police and army
Out of a country now locked in political gridlocks

Out of the lunatic moans of Mugabe against Britain
Out of the lunatic bile of Mugabe against the West
Out of the forthcoming breakdown due to this defiance
Out of cry songs that now stains the whole region
Out of the stench of South Africa's *silent diplomacy*
Out of the stench of SADC and Africa's denial
Out of a conspiring humanity
Out of this chaos is a journey that leads across Limpopo River.

We are footfalls walking through the dense forest
So many frontiers we have crossed

So many shadows of so many at one side
And our silenced dreams on the other side.

The raven's voice falls silent in the darkened leaves
The trees are the only ones who pray for themselves
For the moon always passes on top of them
And in the dark nights we wait for the moon
To tell us to venture into the hungry crocodiles in Limpopo
And I can see their red tongues stretching out
To lick the slime of our yoke and blood.

We are another one among these marauding herds
Limpopo River is now a mixture of silt, blood, bones and scars
Where other traumatised adults giggle chorus of grief
And every anguished cry feed these fat crocodiles
We are now bones within this river's churn
Soon fish will have to negotiate us.

AT BEITBRIBGE BORDER POST

Consider this pinpoint of entry at Beitbridge
And lose control to the neurosis of this border
To paper passports, rubber stamps and ink
That simply professes where one belongs
Consider also the money-mongering border-man
Maybe he is trying to uphold the order of things
Maybe he is trying to survive through this order of things.

The order of things is now more stunning
Than when they were running out of their country
Nobody showed anyone passports, rubber stamps and ink
Entries and exits were at every point
Without this stunning awareness of this border
So time, like water, flows away and is soon forgotten
And the raven shivers into the wind...

From a breathe of a connection
From the brutality of denying this connection
From borders become electric walls
From bonds broken by borders
From standing all day long at border post counters
From standing all day long at home affairs offices

From laws made to make us feel illegal
From eyes which tell which land belongs to which people
From sleeping all night long in tall birch trees
From a pack of hungry lions

From a pack of border-gangsters, hyenas and wild dogs.

The voices are still coming up from the river
The river roars into our ears one song
Of the history of a people who have lost their way
Over and over again.

It is a hammer's job that trampled the place we were born
Our country is now a bleeding wound that cannot contain us
But in the looking we discover the absence of blood
Whilst we stumble along this mad road
Of becoming citizens in another country
And being fully human some day.

So we live in a remembered sorrow
The lost ones are like this- an unborn soul
The ones left alone, humankind's bastard daughter
Just a colourless corpse!

It is an African phenomenon, I tell you
It is the thing that has come out of all of Africa
Like an imitation of an imitation
But always pretending to ourselves
What selves, I ask you
Broken men, broken women, broken children
Broken, broken, broken, broken, broken....

REFUGEES

Even though Eagles always have choices
In the great wide circles
Above and below them
But they never fight the wind!

Out of road bridges, tents and shack-towns
Out of refugee camps and dirty bins
Out of ghost towns
Our ghosts burns inside us without guilt
Out of the neon-glimmer of uptowns
Out of girls become bitches to survive
Out of fear, anger and poisoned hearts
Out of men become killing bastards
Out of the cold shivers of winter nights
Out of fires, floods and lives lost
Out of empty shells, empty lives, and empty beings
Out of traps sprung by the police on foreigners
Out of police trucks ferrying us back to Zimbabwe.

The policeman's gun is pointing at me
His partner is picking on me
Curious animals sniffing for a bribe
This illegal war against immigrants
Breeds unfettered patriotism of citizens against foreigners.

They want to crack our skulls
They want to burn us alive

Laugh and rejoice around our dead
They want to kill every foreigner
Cut cords from our bellies
Suck blood from our corpses
They want to eat our flesh
They want to rape our women
Step on our babies
They want to dig our graves
And burn our bones
That we cannot live anymore
Cannot die again
Cut off in our prime.

Our weakness is an affront to them
Always being quantified, measured
And tagged *Makwerekwere, Makwerekwere.*
Maybe next time they would grind us into flour
Package and distribute us
And I think it would be more-instructive
More efficient, more cost-effective.

VOICES FROM EXILE

From the loneliness of this time
From yesterday, today, tomorrow
From this hour, this minute, this second
From what might have been
From gazing at dreams rotting in the sun
From the need of closure from our illegal ourselves
From time served being refugees but still unwanted
From an echo of ourselves that no longer exist.

This poem is the soft call of one lonely raven
That has lost her loved birth-ones
It is the voice of reason in times of pestilence
It is the voice of the spirit that left luggage
And bundles of bones in Limpopo River
It is the voice of flesh and blood that sustains
Fish and crocodiles in Limpopo
Year in, year out
It is the voice of the badger swallowing in grief
It is the voice of the raccoon chocking in blame.

It maybe is too late for us
To start our own definition
This is not the life we dreamt of
But it is the life we have
For life at this place is called
Everyone's life is a burden
And the raven has left us to our disastrous methods

No one ever listens to us
So give me all your fears
Let me hold all your sorrows in my heart
This poem is yours
To harvest that which has been lost
To smell the heat still rising in our birth place
We are the way to the way it used to be
Foreigners in a new place, still waiting
Waiting for light, space and time

I know you are a whisper, a word, a song
Thrumming in the heartbeat of your own heart
Laughter shouting red blossoms into the wind
Greeting the sun, the moon, the stars
Resounding like ram's horns in the synagogues of our souls
Melodies bridging over the abyss of this suffering
Let's dream together like two wings of the same bird
Being carried away on the shoulder of these notes
Here is my voice that cannot sing to you.

LEADERSHIP

Everlasting leadership
of a born leader.

The leader in control
the led in responsiveness.

They think
and reflect together.
Like sunset on the windows.

THEY MURDER OUR CHILDREN WITH THEIR WEAPONS

Battlefields blooming in blood.
  The country now locked in irons
    of medieval terrors.
      Guzzling, burning-bright blue giant.
       Weapon dealer-
        selling tanks, bombs
        ammunition, used to threaten the masses.
      And douse the country with angry flames.
Is there another way to say this?

Who has done anything to save them?
  Who has heard their protests, their pains?
    their cries, the tears of our children?
    How many poems have we written?
What alarm bell haven't we wrung?

While Africa, UN, and SADC waits, watches
  USA, UK, on the sidelines, this side
    China, Russia and South Africa are
      on the other side.
      Now I realise they won't be no eyes
      no ears, no hands
    no art, no song, no story
no useless poem like this one.

That will bring the country

of our dried tears.
   Or rein back love and laughter
into our children's burning-
silent thirst.

PLUNDER IN MY HEART

One is a surprise.
Two is a surfeit of words.
Three is impossible to process.
But then, somehow- in their cluttered
Thousands--- they have disappeared.
Bruising our sidewalks, a thousand
cells. Where no battle has been.
Where no one sees. Blood
for water- blood fills the
ponds. Plunder in my
heart! Reading
these hiero-
glyphs
have to
wait
For calmer times.

WHAT DEMOCRACY

I have got to be there.
I can't stay away forever.
I have got to see.
what became of my country.

People once voted
and I took an oath.
Vouch to fight rigging of elections.
Deprivation:
and processes there-of.

The people travelled miles to compete
in these elections.
Hunger, anger, poverty, asides.
Fellow citizens, all believing
that late March's spirit will free them
to pay homage to this democracy.

This word is alien!
It is a shadow that impresses decisions.
But has never been experienced.
Always victims to greedy vampires
my people have only smelled death
this is the democracy they know.

THE LATEST

Aftermaths of
garbage tossed about, sewage rotting.

Dirty water, empty stomachs,
empty lives, empty beings.

This garden is
a history of
thousands of them.
Political loose canons
living in the exclusive suburbs.

But in the dusty, populated
Budiriro's streets

Crammed thoughts like bombs are
waiting to explode-

THIS ART OF SUPPRESSION

Now the windows and doors
are closed
in the tea-pot shaped country.
But the battle still rages on.
And the frames are shadowed
by a shell that speaks of death.

A sort of lofty remembrance
in my mind
paints tiny flitting layers of
experience diluting limitation.
Pushing my awareness
into some sort of epiphany.

But can I see, can I smell
with my eye, with my nose
the blood in those battlefields
seemingly so clean of blood?

So finely crafted
this art of suppression
is a work of art!

No outside ear can hear
the thundering guns
flashing knives.
Sounds of henchmen

championing a killing!

Could I sense their obvious pain
their valleys of tears, their cries
their grief-strung hearts
their endless miseries
the path of self destruction
they are now set on?

FATED

This people remains downtrodden
in their hungers, the emptiness-
of their lives.
In their victim's posture!

They scrounge for food in the streets.
Their children are in the streets.
Their women have chosen
a moonlight career.

There is no retirement for this people
like a dappled spider
in the specks of its own webs.
There is no rest for this people.

THE CANARY OF OUR TIME

They say ZANU-PF
          is breaking up
like the arctic ice melting
due to global warming
vanishing into explosive oceans.

They say ZANU-PF
          is breaking up
but hardly no one notices this
except a few newspaper people
using puzzling mirrors.

They say ZANU-PF
          is breaking up
startled by the sight of the in-fighting
disruptions, resignations, cleansing
leaving a lot of people stranded.

They say ZANU-PF
          is breaking up
but they always forget that
a revolutionary party eats itself
in order to rejuvenate its own Napoleon.

41

SIMILARITIES

Mugabe protects himself,
  From western angers-
    By using South Africa.
      As a condom.
        Whilst he kills-
Innocent Zimbabweans.

Just like Zuma-
  Protects himself-
    From corruption charges-
      By using a shower cap and baby oil.
        Whilst he rapes-
Lady-justice South Africa.

MY AXIS OF EVIL

SOUTH AFRICA, CHINA, RUSSIA, VIETNAM, and BURKINA FESO
(for blocking the sanctions resolution on Zimbabwe, especially South Africa for its moral bankruptcy and ineptitude to deal with the Zimbabwean situation, and China for sending arms to Mugabe, the weapons which were used to kill innocent people).

SADC, AU, UN (for their procrastinations and their failure to deal with most of the disturbances in Africa and the whole world).

Mugabe, Mbeki, Motlanthe and Kikitwe (they deserve to get some time at the international court of whatever justice).

Makoni and Mutambara (for the 8% vote that they defrauded the stupid 8% of Zimbabweans who thought they were being very clever, and I am very tempted to include, separately, as a member of my axis of evil, that 8%).

UNISA (Patyana in particular and his Mbeki leadership, whatever leadership that is, school).

Zimbabwe joint operations command, that is POLICE, CHIHURI, CI.O, Defence forces, CHIWENGA, Shiri, Sibanda, Zimhondi, MNANGAGWA, MUTASA, and Sekeramayi).

ZANUPF leadership and the militias.

43

Jonathan Moyo (never, ever could I ever be able to forgive him for what he did to our ZBC, ZIMPAPERS, and to us all), ZIMPAPERS, ZBC (for they totally disgust me).

Chinamasa, Hunzwi, Gezi, and Manyika (that whatever court shouldn't forget this terrible four-some, and Gezi, Hunzwi, and Manyika, must be exhumed from their graves and their bones must be put on trial for the pain they inflicted on Zimbabweans).

ZANUPF supporters, all Zimbabweans wherever there are now, including me, and whilst I am still at Z, I am tempted to include Zuma (for corruption, AIDS denials when he was deputy to the Chief-denialist Mbeki, and for his stupidity, honestly he galls me and reminds me of that ominous pestilence in the Mugabe-form and making. If you were me you would run like I am already doing).

Lastly the international court of whatever justice, for letting the above alone.

PS. I am tempted to include FRANCE, PORTUGAL, for inviting Mugabe to meetings in their countries

PPS. Not to forget USA, UK, Canada, Japan, Australia, Italy, New Zealand, Germany and Japan (for their becoming irritating noises, useless pollution!), and all the other countries in the world, you would think they would do something about it!

One wishes one could emigrate from the entire human race,

death (DYING!),
that too!

FOR NIGEL

In the carnival of a conspiracy
  Words distorting truth to lies.
    Writer in a bloc falls down
      With unexpressed anger.

But a toddler bubbles in-
  Sad iambic pentametric tears.
    In a biographical poem like-
      Free falling operatic comedies.
        That does not keep their laughter.

Nigel, you spent 72 days,
  Locked with your parents
    Colin and Violet, for sins unknown,
      In Chikurubi maximum prison.

But only gamblers-
  Have rushed to your bubble wails.
    Searching for some currents,
      An ode, a ditty, or a sonnet.
        But diving for gold, and leaving you.
          Letting you endure your losses alone.

'VICTORY'S GLORY'

When I see my people
I think of sandworms
  burrowing through the sands
    surfacing once, to test, but continuing
    on their journeys.

  "They are breaching through"
  Someone must have said that.
Cheering the ascending giantworm
springing for another giant leap
sprouting to its highest point.

"The space is opening up."
 The people rejoices
  cheering fresh colours shinning through.
  Reds, blacks, whites, yellows, greens of
  the people's flag colours mixing with
crimson, vermillion, maroon and gold
to form some orange-scarlet of "victory's glory."

A WAR MEMORIAL FOR MUGABE

He never touched a gun.
  Not even in Mozambique.
He never died in a battle.
  Or liberated a prison camp.

He fought the war of leadership.
  Killing rivalries-
Chitepo and Tongogara
Are still unclaimed.

He fought with the generals-
  Of great respect, short mind.
He fought every adjacent difference.
  And the masses he longed for,
  But never understanding them,
  Despised them.

He fought his own wars-
  And there is no medal-
  Nor a memorial for such brutalities.
  There is not even a suitable court to try him.

How could a single man wipe out millions?
  In and outside his country.
  And gorge thousands in daylight,
  For over three decades-
  Whilst the whole world keeps mum.

STATE OF NATION ADDRESS

Over 20 000 people have been infected with cholera
Over 1100 have died by mid-December of cholera
Over 60 000 will be affected by March 2009 and
Over 16 000 deaths!

Number 3 on the list of failed states and a couple
more months
We will beat Somalia to this proud mantle!

8 million need food aid before our next harvest,
which means everyone!

No fertilizers, no pesticides, no agricultural implements,
No rains, no farming done, so it basically means
It's another 12 months of food aid.

No schools, no teachers, no hospitals, no nurses, doctors -
No companies, no work, no money
Nowhere to go, nothing to do, nothing, nothing
No government,

So I have decided to address the nation this year
And this is the state of affairs as we look forward to
Another *"No", New Year.*

XENO(NEGRO)PHOBIA WARNING

How much longer will Motlanthe
allow migrants like hearing a song's end
and see Mugabe's corpses
swarming through Limpopo river.

Corpses scrambling out of Zimbabwe
gasping for fresh air, while South Africans
squirm from this encroaching pestilence.
Some of which makes it to high ground.

But what habitation, what work
will they find? Only a few
melting through to the top.
And the rest, is a frigid motley-lot.

Huddled along the tarred roads.
Waiting for a day's cleaning job
or to fix and fit, load and unload
some rich man's looty-booty.

Crowds standing shoulder to shoulder
under the bright southern sun.
Their browned shaggy bodies
can't support them against ridicule.

Political and economic refugees
migrating into an alien culture.

Where scrambling wars are the norm
and greedy officials feasts upon them.

Now, too far from home.
Doomed to be butchered
by black South Africans' melting impatience
and negrophobia(xenophobia) fangs.

A MUTATED IDENTITY

I have discovered a miniature
a mutation of my people
snuggle in this country
since the old Vereeniging era
fondly known as the Wainera era.

Of our grand-fathers, and fathers
who came long before the hordes
that have crossed lately.

But I do not care enough
to wrap them around me and tie
them to myself.
Not even to transplant
them to my being.

JOHANNESBURG

A town on the far
Away clouds, low-slanted
Light of the south.

And the glow of this town
Is like a window into my past.

But I am now a part
Of this town.

Rejecting
Only the waters in those
Drifting clouds.

THREE GOVERNMENTS

They have tailored three governments
to layer on Zimbabwe's body-politic.
The peak of arrogance and misgovernance
could be the same, either way.
        It is androgynous
                like our life itself.
                        I am tongue-tied
and can't say well the price of suffering
that my generation has seen, will see
either way we go.
There is not much difference.

Mbeki gave us Mugabe, Mutambara, and Tsvangirai.
        And we now have an evil,
                dullard, and fickle government.
                        And we no longer have
a single song of freedom to sing.
Maybe we have to delete ourselves
out of our lives
and maybe come back in another lifetime.
If we could only do that!

WAITING STILL

A song that can sing songs
Of that olden trek

It is like a seed of the past
Waiting for me.

And a little wind has covered
All our tracks.

But I still have this
Soft burning.

And I am kept alive by it
Waiting still.

LIVES NEVER LIVED

Hundreds, thousands, dead with lives
they never lived.
      Tongogara and Chitepo couldn't survive
         the terrors in their voices.
    But they gave us all the gift of a new nation.
    and Mugabe worked as a ray of light
burning through the horrors of the liberation
struggle.

In Matebeleland they died with lives
they never lived.
     The event is still unexplainable.
  The mass graves of tens of thousands overshadowing
       any spirit of reconciliation preached
         at independence.
    Death's gift bringing us once more together
      in the 1987 unity accords.
And to another bout of reconciliation.

But dying they never stopped, with lives
      they never lived.
    Throughout another decade of brutalities.
         Yet they endured!
     While each measured death's pain receded
   from their memories, always replaced
   by another shadow of a reconciliation

and a selflessness of their spirit.

White farmers, and a new party formed, yet they died
                    with lives they never lived.
            Displacements, farm invasions, stolen elections
                        gunshots: police, military and security brutalities.
                    Echoing through the rural area's dark nights and-
suburban light.
With lyrics like the wagging song of
                        the river of blood, singing songs of despair.
                Disenchantment and dismay churning throughout
the whole country, and also
hunger, poverty, diseases and death.

UNEMPLOYMENT'S CHEQUE

This phrase of error---, failure,
has hurried all our endeavours.
And there is no tranquilization,
now needed.

We deal with jagged edges-
of life, willingly.
Without any refuse.

As long as a day passes by-
we survive,
by conjuring a way to disappear-
inside ourselves.

In the evening's dusk.
Its crux collects the remains of-
the painful bits of a long day.

My heart skips a beat-
to the wailing siren down the street.
Lending sound and substance to that fear.

The fear in my heart perhaps-
is what only Mugabe,
can gloss over.

With the flame of the candle gone-

I sit in the gloomy shack,
and cried tears of pain of hunger,
of how young children are dying.

They are just kids---, in poverty!
Tiny, empty stomachs-
Unemployment's cheque!

We are so hungry, not just for food-
but for some fresh thoughts,
to such a freedom.

Depressed, estranged, ungrown sons.
Like spectres of a famous fable, we live,
in crannies where light fails to reach us.

Living in time-speeds,
that reverses computation.
Where ideologues live---,
to wilt and to dissipate---

Under Mugabe's butcheries

Like synaptic connections are unlearned-

And thickened by experience.

We who are older can live-
below our older layers.

59

But we could cry out aloud,
if we could?

MUSE

If they press this mouth's
mute button.
My mind's eye would still have
thoughts flexing unconsciously.

Complex undertows
in my brain's grey box
plunging me deeper and deeper-

Into a solitude of my angers.
Which strips my mind
and envelop me in strangeness.

TALES HIDDEN IN TEARS

I take these words to sleep
  melt them down
    in the dark.

I need to address each word
sedate them
this glow of.

    Inaudible whispers
  in a sea of graves
defining definition.

A limitless silence
in a shadowed light.
Grimaces like smiles?
Laments like songs?

Vulnerable woman
  in the services of their dead
   watching their dead children
    and adhering to their kinsfolk
     with legions of love.

Tales hidden in tears
beneath skies blued
by hurried madness
of the struggles of democracy.

Young men
with bayonets rooming the streets
rushing for another killing
in the absence of
the rule of law.

And the presence of
a mum conspiring humanity.
Jock, I wish I could lock
this door, just lock it.

IN A GHETTO

There have gone under
Boxed by cholera
Buried in the earth
Forgotten, like all the dead.
In a ghetto, in Chitungwiza
Graves tightly packed.
Still fresh, still new.
There lies-
Whose lives were disfigured?
Frayed and effaced
By the sword, his sword.
Taken and consumed by graves
Farms and building space-
In Chitungwiza,
For the burial of the dead.
And they can only touch us-
In dreams, dark dreams-
We feel their tug, our failures.
But they never stay,
Never surfacing.

I SHALL BE MORE HONEST

Birds uses trees as camouflage
Mugabe does the same thing
With revolutionary rhetoric.

Powdering the police, army, and CIO
With food, farms, and money.
Whilst the whole country starves
And dies of cholera.

Mugabe doesn't want us to see
How bad he is.
Africa plays along and acts like
It doesn't know how bad he is.

But when the price of telling-
The truth goes down, then,
I shall be more honest.

COWARDS

The brave ones did not leave
and they stole the show
waving to all from atop.

But we the cowards
knew its safer
from the outside.

But when we begin to whine
of an ache, the ache-
a vibrato in the abysm
of this nothingness.

Wishing for home
we are breaking into small
drops of rains that
might be tears.

The brave ones have
merry-go-rounds
laughing at us the symbols of fear
cowards, cowards, cowards!

DREAMING

Then I hear those bloody green bombers
pursuing me.
In the deep valley of my mind.

And my mind
scrimmaging through centuries-old
runs along, with my body.

Three steps into a motionless interior
before I am captured.

They beat me throughout this night
as they circle me
in a centuries-old spear dance.

Until the day-dreamer's blue hour
brought me here to this moment.

WHO SHALL ACT FOR ZIMBABWEANS

Mangwana (you would wonder which morning, tomorrow?),
now is a new morning for that loudmouth, cholera denialist
Ndlovu (elephant) at publicity, publishing...

Lies and misinforming especially the laughing stock British
and their gullible cousins across the Atlantic, apologising
about Mugabe's gaffes on Cholera in Zimbabwe

"There is no cholera in Zimbabwe"
"It is Britain's biological warfare against our loved nation"
"Ha, ha, ha, Mugabe was only joking and making fun at the British"

Sekeramayi (laughing at your mother, or for mother, whichever!),
now laughs for Midzi (roots), mixing and mining roots, diamonds
with the Mujurus (the termites) at Mines and mining development
ministry

Chigwedere (shacking knees, kneeling, whatever that means)
continues un-educating or mis-educating whatever schools
and pupils left in Zimbabwe, and sometimes un-sporting sport
and un-culturating a cultureless education sport and culture
ministry he had once rejected for a Seke chieftainship job.

Mushove (WHATS THAT!), still acts at transport, transporting us,
shoving us back to pre-communication era. Chinamasa survives
once again, and now is at finance, replacing, or is it acting for
Mbengegwi. Mbengegwi, not that beardo at foreign affairs,

68

for I know this one a little better

I haven't forgotten that day you agued
for almost two hours for your 2*T35 Mazda trucks.
Now it makes sense why you felt, then,
that you didn't have to pay, not even
a single cent, useless change to you.
That buffoon was Mr Zimbabwe's money bag then.
So, according to him, he deserved to get them free.

Free, free, free things-
it is the hall mark of the world of
Mad Bob Republic, thatta boy.
Now they each have a free ministry
to bleed out gazillions of Zimkwachas
and farfillions of the coveted US$ and Rands
That Gono, steal, another boy-
from anti-retroviral funds and programmes.

Whilst Mugabe elects himself and acts
as the President, Prime minister, and
the Parliament, in the absence of
Tsvangirai who now acts as Zimbabwe's
ambassador to Botswana.
At least with no passport of his own.
But who shall act for Zimbabweans
with nowhere to go?

COMING HOME

This hardened silence, I see more
than I wish to see, and can no longer
recognise my own landscape.
For there is too much silence-
a hung-up kind of silence.

Strolling along the road
from the bus-stop to home.
I recall how we used
to roughshod all over this landscape.
In our childhood and teenage years.

And of my friend Thomas
who stayed behind
to study the twist and turns
on the map of our country.
Thinking that he was right on time!

But this day, without a map
I walk home
and sit on the cement bench
that surrounds the better half
of my mother's kitchen
and had a plateful of Sadza.

Although the Sadza here

is still as good as I remember
so much has changed.
Except for Nyanga Mountain
still redolent in the horizons
reflecting in its rainbows.

I saw Mother, Father, Sister, Brother
and my long seen Cousins, Aunts, Uncles
I have dreamt seeing for eons
of eating sad soul music and inspired
melancholies down south.

But I did not see Thomas
neither his portrait in the processes
nor his delicious naps under
the kitchen's sweet shade.

The kitchen's doors were opening and closing
always watching, waiting for him.
Maybe Thomas was now enjoying another
moment's time--- a waiting silence?

I was later told that he had developed
Anger inside his heart
and that he ran and ran on roads
away from what he didn't know
in his heart, and that
he kept saying the demon's name
and paid the price of a broken will

and vanished into the depths.

But tomorrow I will go to the meadowlands.
May the wide meadowlands still be there?
For me, unlike Thomas.
That borders on those north knolls
which seemed so small, so sweet, so soothing
like when we were small and chasing rainbows.

The rush of these memories
greying with this day.
Realising another irreplaceable loss
of some fine company.
Leaving me again in sadness.

SAID AND UNSAID

We remember the uprootings
the tear trails, bloodtrails
blood stained ribs bleeding
short breaths-
of the dying.

This war nature
has not breathed
flowers into our hearts
but fiery flowering Judases
with a decaying halo.

Do we always have to use
a loaded gun
to settle our differences?
What has been the price of this victory?
if not sands in our hearts?

And if we try to sweep the sands
out of our dead hearts.
The dead of our deadened hearts
spits out goblets of blackened sand-blood.

Though freedom is a joyous thing
now it has a hallow ring.
The images within it

both said and unsaid that-

We can't abide a path
of least resistance anymore.
We have to walk directly into the unblinking
muzzle flash of a gun again.

The bullets zinging and zinning
through our bodies.
Through whatever little dreams
now left in us.

Printed in the United States
By Bookmasters